Balboa Press books may be ordered through booksellers or by contacting:

Balboa Press
A Division of Hay House
1663 Liberty Drive
Bloomington, IN 47403
www.balboapress.com
1 (877) 407-4847

ISBN: 978-1-9822-3020-3 (sc)
ISBN: 978-1-9822-3019-7 (e)

Library of Congress Control Number: 2019908320

Print information available on the last page.

Balboa Press rev. date: 06/28/2019

BALBOA
PRESS
A DIVISION OF HAY HOUSE

Mi abuelita
My Grandma

Dedicatoria: a mi Grema, una guerrera, por su amor incondicional.

~~~~~~~~~~~~~~~~~~~~~~~~~~~~~~~~~

Dedication: to my Grandma, a warrior, for her unconditional love.

Mi abuelita me enseñó a amar. Me enseñó a jugar, a comer y a estudiar. También me enseñó a cuidar mi corazón. Me decía que con los sentimientos no se juega.

~~~~~~~~~~~~~~~~~~~~~~~~~~~~~~~~

My grandmother taught me what love is. She taught me how to play, how to eat and how to study. She also taught me how to take care of my heart. She would tell me that feelings are not to be joked about.

De niña, mi abuelita me cuidaba. Me hacía licuados por la mañana para que no me fuera a la escuela con hambre y para que pudiera aprender algo nuevo.

—————

As a child, my grandmother would take care of me. She would make me breakfast smoothies so I wouldn't go to school hungry and so I could learn something new.

También me lavaba y planchaba la ropa y el uniforme para que fuera presentable a la escuela. Para ella, mi educación era muy importante.

She also washed and ironed my clothes and my school uniform to be presentable at school. For her, my education was very important.

Mi abuelita cantaba por las mañanas mientras escuchaba la radio. Ella siempre estaba feliz. También cortaba guayabas para mí de nuestro árbol.

My grandma sang for me all mornings while listening to the radio. She was always happy. She also reached for guavas for me from our backyard tree.

Cuando yo tenía frío, mi abuelita me abrazaba con su rebozo. Cuando estaba enferma, me daba medicina. Cuando lloraba, me consolaba.

~~~~~~~~~~~~~~~~~~~~~~~~~~~~~~~~~

When I felt cold, my grandmother covered me with her shawl. When I felt sick, she gave me medicine. When I cried, she comforted me.

Cuando tenía hambre, me hacía una sopa de fideo. Cuando tenía sed, me hacía agua fresca.

~~~~~~~~~~~~~~~~~~~~~~~~~~~~~~~~~~~

When I was hungry, she would make me soup. When I was thirsty, she would make fruit punch.

Las abuelitas son personas muy especiales en la vida de los niños, las abuelitas son personas muy importantes. Es importante aprender de ellas y disfrutarlas.

In the lives of all children, grandmas are very important. It is important to learn from them and enjoy spending time with them.

Las abuelitas cuentan historias de cuando ellas eran niñas. Ellas son sabias. Escúchalas y aprende de sus historias. La historia de ellas también es la tuya.

Grandma's tell stories about their childhood. They are wise. Listen to them and learn from their stories. Their story is also yours.

¿Cómo se llama tu abuelita? ¿Te gusta jugar con ella? ¿Qué te enseña ella? ¿La ves o hablas con ella con frecuencia?

What is your grandma's name? Do you enjoy playing with her? What does she teach you? Do you see her or speak with her often?

¿Alguna vez has dibujado a tu abuelita? ¿De qué color es su cabello? ¿Qué le gusta comer o beber? ¿Lo sabes?

Have you ever drawn your grandma? What is the color of her hair? What does she like to eat or drink? Do you know?

¿Qué es lo que más te gusta de tu abuelita? ¿Se lo has dicho alguna vez?

What do you like the most about your grandma? Have you ever shared that with her?

Las abuelitas son un regalo de la naturaleza. Dale a tu abuelita muchos abrazos y besos cuando la veas.

~~~~~~~~~~~~~~~~~~~~~~~~~~~~~

Grandmas are a gift from nature. Give your grandma lots of hugs and kisses when you see her.

Printed in the United States
By Bookmasters